discovermore

Earth's Processes

What Is Plate Tectonics?

Doug Bradley

Britannica Educational Publishing

IN ASSOCIATION WITH

THE ROSEN PUBLISHING GROUP

Published in 2027 by Britannica Educational Publishing (a trademark of Encyclopædia Britannica, Inc.) in association with The Rosen Publishing Group, Inc.
2544 Clinton Street, Buffalo, NY 14224

Distributed exclusively by Rosen Publishing.
To see additional Britannica Educational Publishing titles, go to rosenpublishing.com.

Editor: Greg Roza
Book Design: Deanna Lepovich

Photo Credits: Cover; (series background) Dai Yim/Shutterstock.com; cover katerina12605/Shutterstock.com; pp. 4, 7, 8 GraphicsRF.com/Shutterstock.com; p. 5 Julia Mountain Photo/Shutterstock.com; p. 6 Albert Stephen Julius/Shutterstock.com; p. 9 dixkom/Shutterstock.com; p. 11 (top) BlueRingMedia/Shutterstock.com; p. 11 (bottom) reisezielinfo/Shutterstock.com; p. 12 Ningaloo.gg/Shutterstock.com; p. 13 Everett Collection/Shutterstock.com; pp. 14, 21, 23 Peter Hermes Furian/Shutterstock.com; p. 15 Wirestock Creators/Shutterstock.com; p. 16 VectorMine/Shutterstock.com; p. 17 Doga Ayberk Demir/Shutterstock.com; pp. 18, 19 Designua/Shutterstock.com; p. 20 BSTOCKVIDEO/Shutterstock.com; p. 21 (inset) imageBROKER.com/Shutterstock.com; p. 22 Metragnome Images/Shutterstock.com; p. 24 Danita Delimont/Shutterstock.com; p. 25 Olenia/Shutterstock.com; p. 26 Alfred Wegener ca.1924-30/Wikimedia Commons; p. 27 Breck P. Kent/Shutterstock.com; p. 29 (top) Frans Delian/Shutterstock.com; p. 29 (bottom) 365 Focus Photography/Shutterstock.com.

Cataloging-in-Publication Data

Names: Bradley, Doug, 1971-.
Title: What is plate tectonics? / Doug Bradley.
Description: New York : Britannica Educational Publishing, in association with Rosen Educational Services, 2027. | Series: Discover more: Earth's processes | Includes glossary and index.
Identifiers: ISBN 9781641906111 (library bound) | ISBN 9781641906104 (pbk) | ISBN 9781641906128 (ebook)
Subjects: LCSH: Plate tectonics--Juvenile literature.
Classification: LCC QE511.4 B656 2027 | DDC 551.136--dc23

Printed in China

Some of the images in this book illustrate individuals who are models. The depictions do not imply actual situations or events.

CPSIA Compliance Information: Batch #QSBRIT27. For further information contact Rosen Publishing at 1-800-237-9932.

Contents

Earth's Puzzle Pieces

Earth's surface isn't just one big piece of land. It's covered in plates that are slowly moving. Earth is covered in a rigid outer layer, called the lithosphere. Under the lithosphere is a soft layer of melted rock called the asthenosphere. The lithosphere is broken up into about a dozen large plates and several small plates. These plates move slowly, only about 2 to 4 inches (5 to 10 cm) per year.

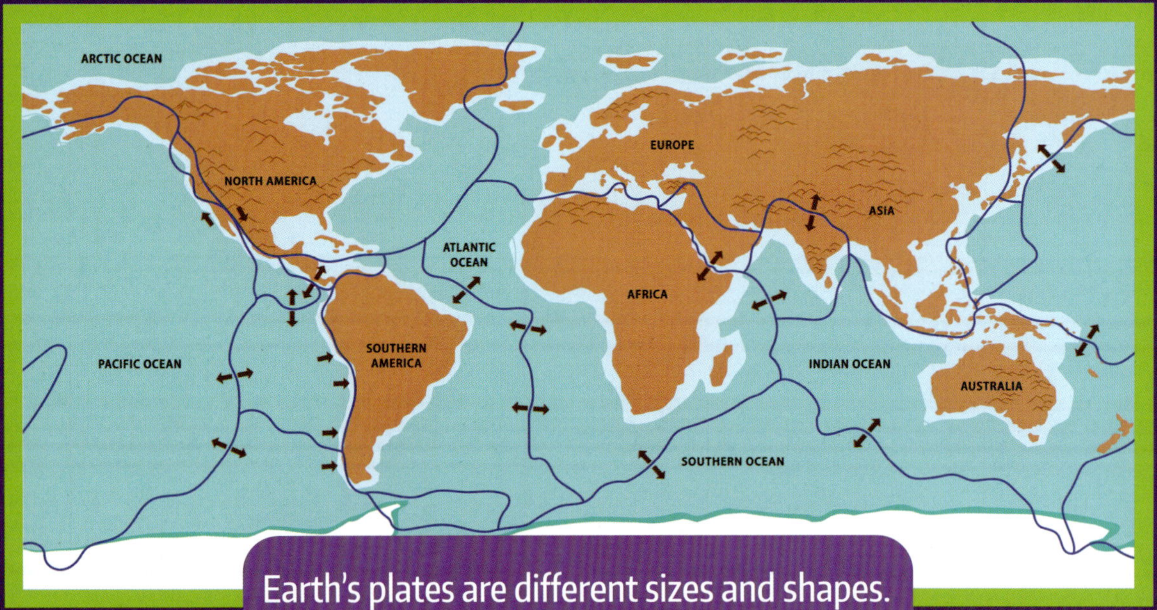

Earth's plates are different sizes and shapes. They fit together like puzzle pieces.

The Himalayas are Earth's largest mountain system. They were formed by plate movement.

The movements of these plates have a huge effect on our planet. Sudden plate movements can cause earthquakes. The movements of the plates can also form mountains and volcanoes. Over long spans of time, the movement of the plates—known as plate tectonics—can change the shape of continents and oceans. Scientists study plate tectonics to better understand Earth's past and how Earth's plates can affect people in the future.

Consider This

How long do you think it takes for mountains to form? Hundreds of years? Thousands? Millions?

Inside Earth

The top layer of Earth is called the crust. The crust is thinner under the oceans than it is under the continents. Under the continents it averages about 19 miles (30 km) thick. Underneath the crust is the more compact rock of the mantle, on which the crust basically floats. The mantle is much thicker, about 1,800 miles (2,900 km). The temperature at the lower part of the mantle is about 6,700°F (3,700°C). The rock there is soft and can move slowly. Below the mantle is Earth's core. The outer part of the core is liquid, while the center of the core is solid.

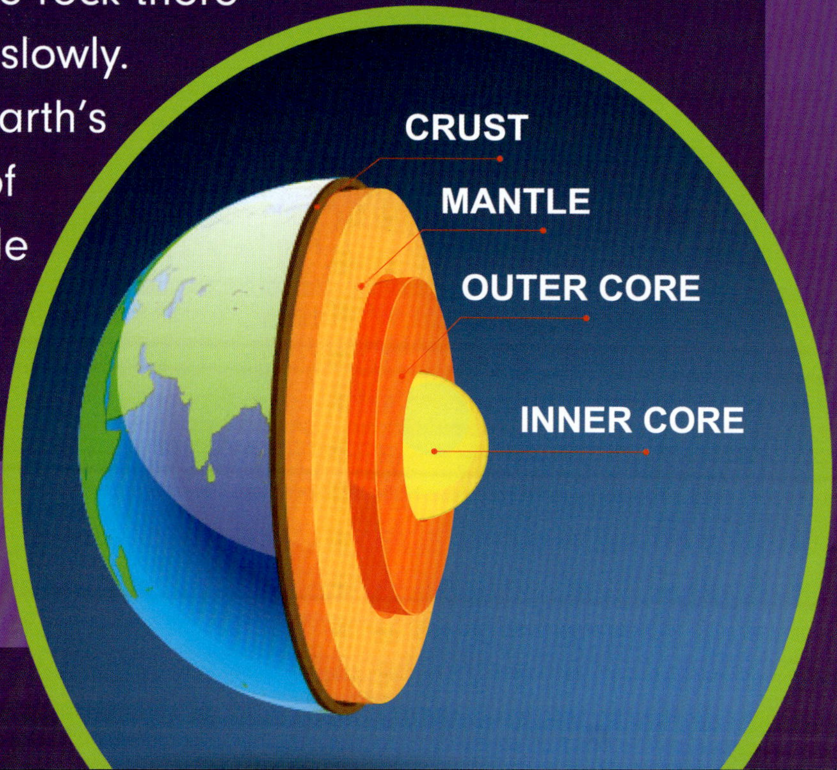

This diagram shows Earth's layers. The crust is by far the thinnest layer.

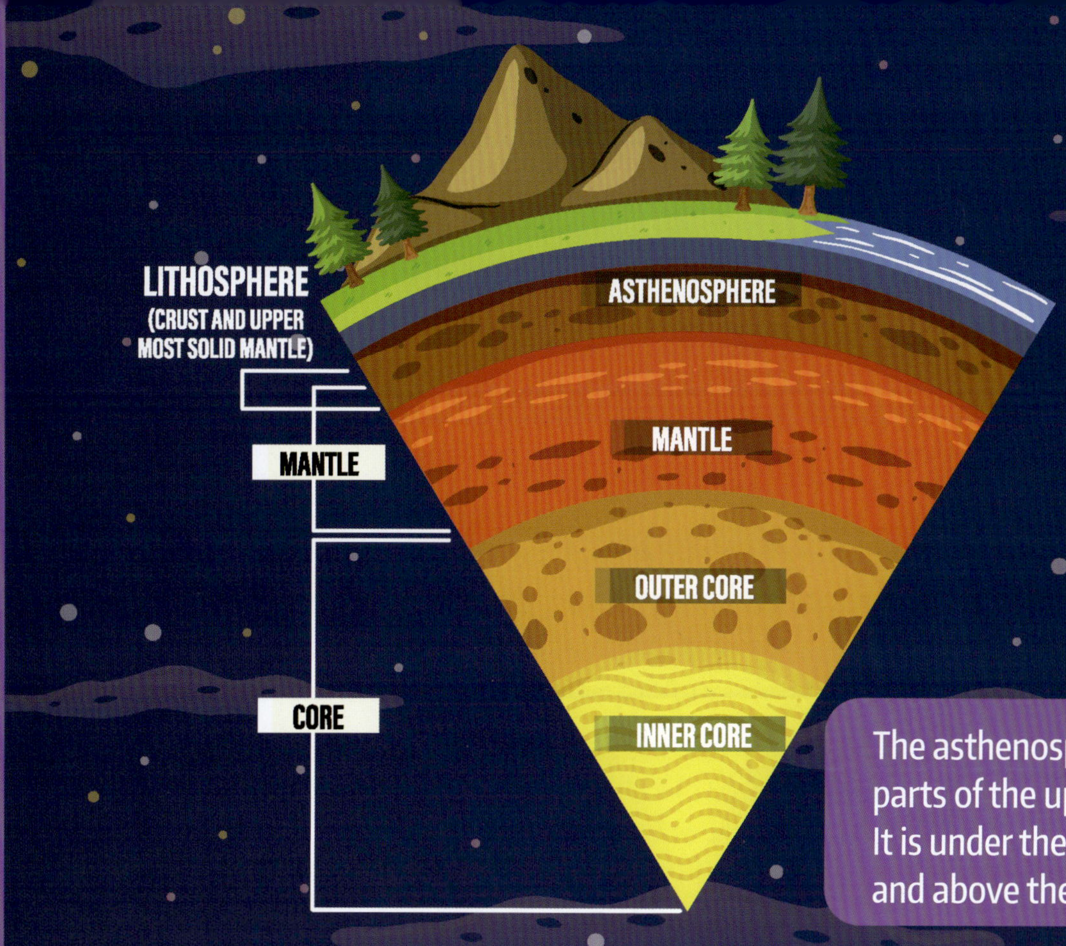

The asthenosphere includes parts of the upper mantle. It is under the lithosphere and above the lower mantle.

The lithosphere consists of the crust and the rigid upper mantle. The asthenosphere is the partially **molten** zone in the mantle, between 60 and 400 miles (100 and 650 km) below the surface. The molten rock allows tectonic plates to slide over the asthenosphere.

WORD WISE

MOLTEN MEANS MELTED, OR LIQUID. IT TAKES A LOT OF HEAT AND PRESSURE TO CREATE MOLTEN ROCK.

Drifting Apart

With all the plates drifting, they inevitably interact with each other in several ways. One way is to move away from each other. Plates that move apart are said to have a **divergent** boundary. When plates move apart they make a crack between them. When a crack opens up on the seafloor, magma rises up and fills in the crack. This is called seafloor spreading. This process can cause earthquakes in the ocean as the seafloor cracks, fills in, and cracks again.

When two plates move away from each other, the space between them fills with magma, which hardens to form new land.

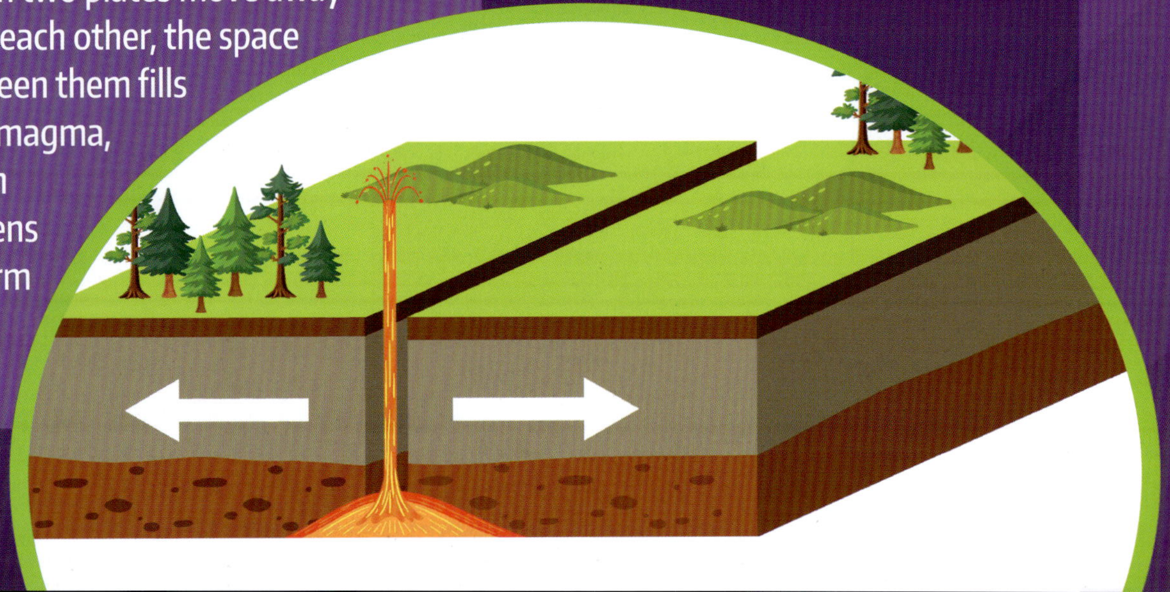

This photograph shows the divergent boundary between the North American plate and the Eurasian plate in Iceland. Iceland sits at the north end of the Marianas Trench, the deepest undersea canyon on Earth!

Divergent boundaries can also exist on land and can create cracks in Earth's surface. These cracks are called rift valleys. The longest rift on Earth's surface is called the Great Rift Valley. It is about 4,000 miles (6,400 km) long with an average width of 30 to 40 miles (50 to 65 km). The rift starts in the Middle Eastern country Jordan and goes south to the African country Mozambique.

WORD WISE

DIVERGENT MEANS MOVING IN DIFFERENT DIRECTIONS, OR MOVING AWAY FROM EACH OTHER.

Crashing Together

Convergent boundaries are between plates that are moving toward each other. Usually, one of the plates is forced underneath the other one. When this happens, the area around the two plates is called a subduction zone. There is a plate in the Pacific Ocean, the Nazca Plate, that is pushing under a plate that makes up South America. As the Nazca Plate pushes under the South American plate, it presses into the hot mantle and melts rock, making magma. The magma rises up and causes volcanoes on the Andes Mountains to form. This type of plate movement can also cause powerful earthquakes.

When two plates on a continent converge, they create mountains and volcanoes. That is how the Himalayas, the highest mountains in the world, were created. If two plates converge under the ocean, they can create volcanic islands. That is how the Mariana Islands in the western Pacific Ocean formed.

The Andes in South America is the longest mountain range in the world. They run through the countries of Venezuela, Colombia, Ecuador, Peru, Bolivia, Argentina, and Chile.

compareandcontrast

The Andes and the Himalayas were formed by convergence. How might the way they formed have affected their length or height?

Volcanic Eruptions at Subduction Zones

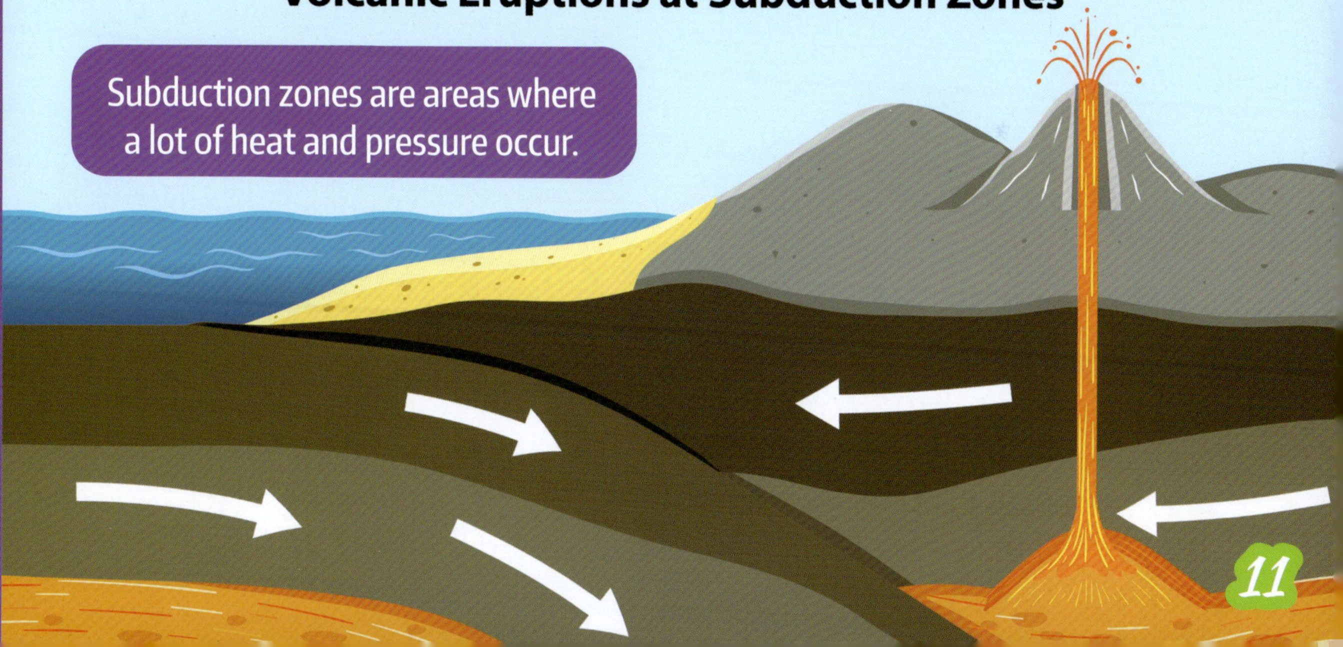

Subduction zones are areas where a lot of heat and pressure occur.

Sliding By

The plates that make up transform faults slide past each other. They do not push into each other or move away from each other. Sometimes, the plates stick together and then slip. This causes earthquakes. Most transform faults are found on the ocean floor. Some, such as the San Andreas Fault in California, appear on continents.

The San Andreas Fault is a transform fault in California that marks the boundary between the Pacific plate and the North American plate.

The San Francisco earthquake of 1906 was one of the most destructive natural disasters in U.S. history. It left more than 250,000 people homeless.

The San Andreas Fault is more than 800 miles (1,300 km) long. The movement of the plates along the fault has caused several major earthquakes. A strong earthquake damaged much of the city of San Francisco in 1906. Another strong earthquake struck the San Francisco area in 1989. Most of the population of California lives near the San Andreas Fault. Some cities and towns are built on top of the fault. Because of the fault, minor earthquakes and tremors are common in California. Buildings, roads, and bridges have been designed to withstand the force of an earthquake.

Consider This

The 1906 earthquake in San Francisco destroyed about 80 percent of the city. The 1989 earthquake was much less devastating. What do you think the city of San Fransico did to be better prepared for earthquakes?

The Ring of Fire

Most volcanoes form along the boundaries of tectonic plates. They can be found on convergent boundaries and divergent boundaries. There are more than 1,500 volcanoes on Earth that could be active. Almost 90 percent of those volcanoes are located in the Pacific Ring of Fire. This is a chain of volcanoes that surrounds the Pacific Ocean. It lies along the edges of the giant Pacific Plate. As the plate moves, it creates earthquakes and volcanoes.

The Ring of Fire is home to about 90 percent of all volcanoes on Earth

Mauna Loa, shown here, is one of five volcanoes that make up the Island of Hawaii.

While most volcanoes are found along tectonic plate boundaries, some are not. Some volcanoes can be found toward the center of tectonic plates. These volcanoes form over what scientists call a hot spot. A hot spot is an area where heat pushes up from Earth's mantle and melts the rock, creating magma, at the base of the lithosphere. The magma then pushes up through the crust, making volcanoes. The Hawaiian Islands were created this way.

Consider This

Mauna Loa is a seamount, meaning it's a mountain that forms on the ocean floor. This makes it one of the largest volcanoes on Earth!

Shake It Up!

Most earthquakes are so small that people cannot feel them. Sometimes, larger earthquakes happen and they can cause serious damage. Most earthquakes are caused by the movement of tectonic plates. When plates move in relation to each other, they build up pressure. When the pressure becomes too great, the plates can move suddenly. This causes an earthquake. The energy is released in the form of shock waves. The waves spread through the rock in all directions. In the most powerful quakes, people thousands of miles away from the center of the quake can feel the ground shake.

Scientists use scales such as this one to show earthquake magnitude, or how strong they are. Some cause little or no damage. Some are highly destructive.

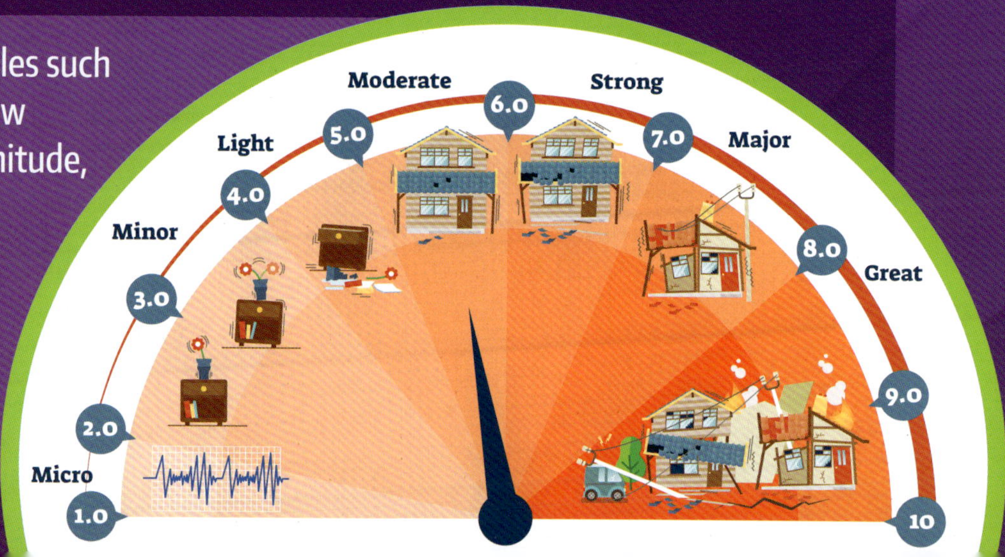

A major earthquake happened in Türkiye in 2023 and caused widespread damage.

Earthquakes can do great damage to buildings, bridges, railroads, and other structures. The violent shaking during earthquakes often causes other problems as well, such as **avalanches**. Tsunamis are huge ocean waves caused by underwater earthquakes that can reach shore and cause great destruction.

WORD WISE

AVALANCHES ARE LARGE AMOUNTS OF SNOW AND ICE THAT FALL DOWN A MOUNTAINSIDE OR CLIFF.

Plates in the Past

Earth's plates have been traveling across the planet's surface for hundreds of millions of years. As the plates move, the continents on them move, too. This movement is called continental drift. The movement of the tectonic plates has changed the shape, size, and location of the continents.

The arrows on this map show the ways in which the different plates are moving.

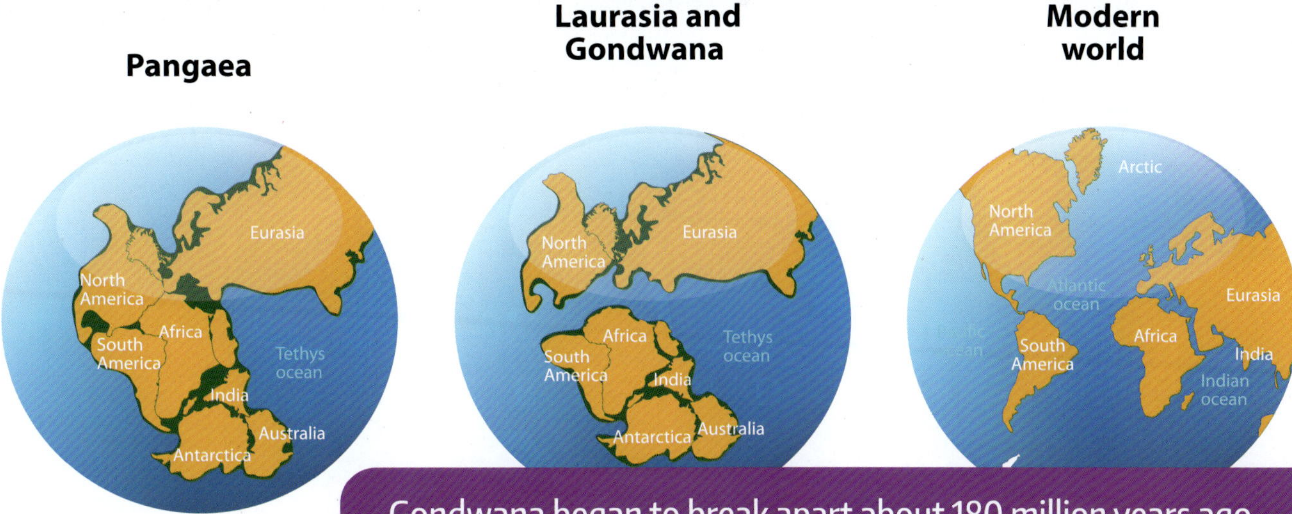

Gondwana began to break apart about 180 million years ago. Laurasia broke apart about 50 million years ago.

About 255 million years ago, nearly all the land on Earth formed one enormous continent called Pangaea. This "supercontinent" began to break apart about 237 million years ago. By about 150 million years ago, it had separated into two large landmasses, Laurasia in the north and Gondwana in the south. Laurasia was made up of the land that is now North America, Europe, and much of Asia. Gondwana included what are now South America, Africa, Australia, Antarctica, India, and Arabia. Later, Laurasia and Gondwana split into pieces.

Consider This

The North American plate is huge! It also moves up to 1 inch (3 cm) a year. What do you think keeps North America moving west?

Scientists believe that there have been several supercontinents throughout Earth's long history. They think that it takes about 500 million years for all the continents to join together into one big continent and then break apart again. The continents continue to move today. Scientists believe that in about 250 million years they will join together again.

Scientists think a supercontinent called Pannotia existed 600 million years ago. It may have looked like this.

Scientists have also found matching dinosaur tracks in the South American country of Brazil and the African country of Cameroon. They were made 120 million years ago when a narrow strip of land still connected the two landmasses.

The idea of continental drift is an old one. It was first suggested to explain why the shapes of the continents looked like they would fit together well. Besides the shape of the continents, there is much evidence supporting the idea that the continents were once united. Most of the evidence is based on the study of ancient climates and the matching of **fossils**, rocks, and geological structures on land separated by huge oceans. For example, the coasts of South America and Africa seem like they could fit together. But scientists have also discovered the fossils of swimming reptiles called mesosaurs on both coasts, further linking their pasts together.

WORD WISE

FOSSILS ARE THE REMAINS OF PLANTS AND ANIMALS THAT LIVED LONG AGO.

Evolution and Climate

The slowly shifting continent shapes and locations has had an effect on the evolution of plants and animals. As the continents moved apart, the diversity, or differences, among plants and animals increased. This is because the spaces that opened up between the continents were filled in with ocean. That meant the plants and animals on different continents could not interact. This is why the animals that live in Australia, like kangaroos, are so different from the animals in North America, like grizzly bears.

Kangaroos only live on the continent of Australia because there was no way for them to travel to other continents.

The Isthmus of Panama is within the country of Panama. The Panama Canal crosses the isthmus.

However, the movement of the plates had the opposite effect about three million years ago. At about that time, volcanic activity in the Pacific Ocean created a land bridge between North America and South America. This land bridge formed the **Isthmus** of Panama. Before that, the two continents were separated. This bridge allowed animals to migrate between the two continents.

WORD WISE

AN ISTHMUS IS A NARROW STRIP OF LAND CONNECTING TWO LARGER LAND AREAS.

Many animals from North America migrated south. Among those animals were many carnivorous, or meat-eating, animals. These carnivores caused the extinction of some animals on the southern continent. Some southern animals, like the armadillo and opossum, migrated north.

Tectonic plates and their movements have also caused extinctions. About 299 to 252 million years ago, a series of extinction events happened. About 70 percent of land animals became extinct, and about 95 percent of marine animals became extinct. Scientists think this was caused by the formation of Pangaea, volcanic activity, and temperature changes.

There are 20 species of armadillo. The nine-banded armadillo is the only species found in the United States.

As Pangea broke apart, ocean water rushed in to fill the spaces, causing new currents to form.

Pangea

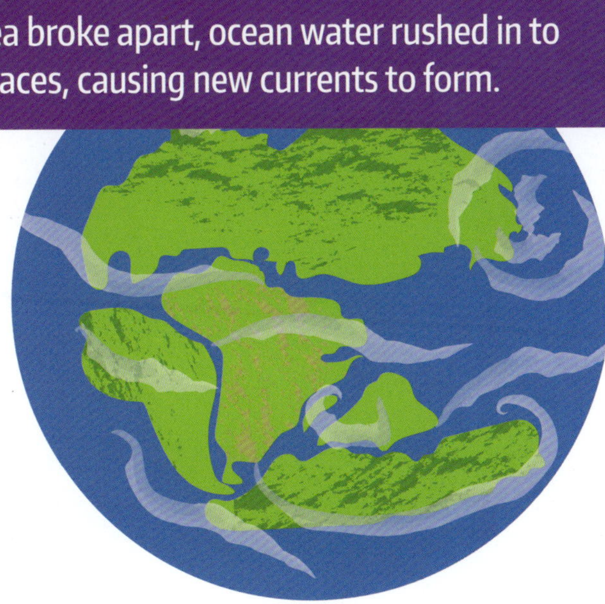

Laurasia
Gondwana

The breakup of Pangaea also had a big effect on Earth's climate. A lot of the climate on Earth has to do with ocean currents and wind. When Pangaea existed, it was completely surrounded by an ocean, called Panthalassa. As Pangaea split apart, the ocean filled in the gaps. This changed ocean currents and resulted in warm and cold water spreading into different areas.

Consider This

Why might carnivores that are new to an area cause the extinction of some animals?

A Little History

In 1912, German scientist Alfred Wegener suggested that all of the continents were once joined together in a supercontinent he called Pangea. He thought that Pangaea split and the pieces drifted apart over long periods of time. He called this idea continental displacement. His **theory** is now called continental drift. Other scientists rejected Wegener's idea because he could not explain how the continents moved.

Wegener was an astronomer. He was also interested in the topic of paleoclimatology—the study of Earth's climates in the distant past.

Glossopteris plant fossils, shown here, have been found in many of the areas that were part of southern Pangea. This discovery supports the idea of continental drift.

In 1929, British geologist Arthur Holmes proposed that the heat from Earth's mantle caused continental drift. His idea received little attention at the time. In the 1960s, however, a number of scientists used the ideas of Holmes and Wegener. They monitored earthquakes and looked at similar fossils from different continents. By doing all of that, the scientists were able to find evidence of plates and their movements, leading to the modern theory of plate tectonics.

WORD WISE

A SCIENTIFIC THEORY IS AN EXPLANATION FOR WHY THINGS WORK OR HOW THINGS HAPPEN.

The Future of Plate Tectonics

Plate tectonics will continue to change the shape of the continents and oceans over the course of hundreds of millions of years. Most of the time, this slow movement doesn't affect our lives. However, when plates suddenly come together, slide against each other, or move apart, serious disasters can occur. Scientists think that it is only a matter of time before another large earthquake happens in California. The San Andreas Fault has been building up pressure for a long time there.

In the last decades, devastating tsunamis have occurred in Japan and Indonesia. The huge waves were caused by earthquakes. The earthquakes were triggered by plates on the ocean floor sliding under each other. The idea of earthquakes and tsunamis is scary. But scientists are improving how they monitor the movement of Earth's plates. This allows scientists to warn people about dangerous events before they occur.

The 2004 Indian Ocean earthquake was an undersea megathrust that created a massive tsunami. Waves up to 100 feet (30.5 m) tall smashed into the coasts of many countries around the Indian Ocean.

compareandcontrast

The threats from earthquakes and tsunamis can be devastating. How are those threats different? How are they similar?

This sign on a beach in Japan warns beachgoers of the danger of earthquakes and tsunamis.

Glossary

asthenosphere The layer of soft, molten rock that lies under the lithosphere.

boundary The dividing line or edge between things.

climate The average weather conditions of a particular place or region over a period of years.

converge To tend or move toward one point or one another.

displacement Movement from one position to another.

evolution An explanation for how all the kinds of living things that exist today developed from earlier types.

extinction The state or process of dying out completely.

fault A break in Earth's crust accompanied by a displacement of rock masses parallel to the break.

geological Having to do with rocks and the history of rocks.

lithosphere The solid, outer part of Earth, consisting of the crust and part of the mantle.

magma Hot, melted rock material within Earth.

migrate To move from one country, place, or location to another.

shock wave A tall wave caused by a shock (as from an earthquake or explosion) to the material through which the wave travels.

subduction The process in which one tectonic plate is forced beneath the edge of another plate.

tremor A small movement of the ground before or after an earthquake.

tsunami A great sea wave produced especially by an earthquake or volcanic eruption under the sea.

volcano A vent in Earth's crust from which melted or hot rock and steam come out.

For More Information

Books

Berry, Alexandria. *Landscapes Long Ago*. Mankato, MN: Cherry Lake Publishing, 2026.

Murray, Julie. *San Francisco Earthquake*. Minneapolis, MN: ABDO Publishing, 2023.

Websites

Plate Tectonics
www.ducksters.com/science/earth_science/plate_tectonics.php
Learn more about continental drift from Ducksters.

2004 Indian Ocean Earthquake and Tsunami
kids.kiddle.co/2004_Indian_Ocean_earthquake_and_tsunami
Read about the 2004 Indian Ocean earthquake and the resulting tsunami.

Index